the
Weekend
Crafter®

Gourd
Crafts

the
Weekend
Crafter®

Gourd Crafts

~~~~~~

20 Great Projects to Dye, Paint, Carve, Bead, and Woodburn in a Weekend

GINGER SUMMIT

LARK BOOKS

A Division of Sterling Publishing Co., Inc.
New York

*This book
is dedicated
to my wonderful
gourd friends
and mentors,
Jim Story and
Virginia Umberger.*

Library of Congress Cataloging-in-Publication Data
Summit, Ginger.
  Gourd crafts : from bowls to birdhouses, 20 great projects to dye, cut, carve, bead, and woodburn in a weekend / Ginger Summit.
     p. cm. -- (Weekend crafter)
  Includes index.
  ISBN 1-57990-152-2
  1. Gourd craft. I. Title. II. Series.
TT873.5.S88   2000
745.5--dc21

                                                      99-41990

                                                      CIP

10 9 8 7 6 5

Published by Lark Books, a division of
Sterling Publishing Co., Inc.
387 Park Avenue South, New York, N.Y. 10016

© 2000, Ginger Summit

Distributed in Canada by Sterling Publishing,
c/o Canadian Manda Group, One Atlantic Ave., Suite 105
Toronto, Ontario, Canada M6K 3E7

Distributed in the U.K. by:
Guild of Master Craftsman Publications Ltd.
Castle Place, 166 High Street, Lewes East Sussex, England BN7 1XU
Tel: (+ 44) 1273 477374, Fax: (+ 44) 1273 478606,
Email: pubs@thegmcgroup.com, Web: www.gmcpublications.com

Distributed in Australia by Capricorn Link (Australia) Pty Ltd.
P.O. Box 704, Windsor, NSW 2756 Australia

If you have questions or comments about this book, please contact:
Lark Books
67 Broadway
Asheville, NC 28801
(828) 236-9730

Printed in China

ISBN 1-57990-152-2

EDITOR:
DEBORAH MORGENTHAL

ART DIRECTOR & PRODUCTION:
DANA IRWIN

PHOTOGRAPHY:
SANDRA STAMBAUGH
(project photos)

RICHARD HASSELBERG
(how-to and gallery photos)

ILLUSTRATIONS & PRODUCTION ASSISTANT:
HANNES CHAREN

ASSISTANT EDITOR:
CATHARINE SUTHERLAND

CONTENTS

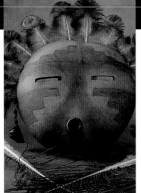

6 ....**Introduction**

G o u r d   B a s i c s :

8 ....What is a Gourd?

10 ....Preparing the Gourd for Crafting

15 ....Surface Treatments for Decorating the Gourd

P r o j e c t s :

22 ....Simple Fruits and Vegetables

24 ....Flowerpots with Upholstery Tacks

26 ....Southwest-Style Mask

28 ....Mexican Painted Dippers

31 ....Santa Claus Figure

34 ....Simple Candleholders

36 ....Lidded Container with Painted Bird

39 ....Mother Goose Birdhouse

43 ....Tortilla Warmer

46 ....Scorched Tea Cups

48 ....Branded Bracelets

51 ....Woodburned Bowls

54 ....Leaf Motif Luminaria

57 ....Pedestal Bowl with Decoupage Lining

60 ....Carved Vase

62 ....Relief Carved Bowl

65 ....Handled Basked with Leather Trim

67 ....Miniature Pots with Knotless Netting

69 ....Gourd with Pine Needle Coiling

71 ....African Bead Shekerie

74 ....**Gallery**

77 ....**Contributing Artists**

78 ....**Acknowledgments**

79 ....**Index**

INTRODUCTION

than expected or less interesting after the first few projects. Another stumbling block for many people as they embark on a new craft is the time and patience it takes to learn a new skill; classes, books, and patterns are hurdles that must be navigated before the newly inspired crafter can actually produce a piece of which to be proud.

Gourd craft offers a refreshing change to all that. No special tools are required to get started—saws from the workbench, scrapers and spoons from the kitchen drawer, shoe polish from the closet, along with pine needles, leather scraps, or leftover yarn and beads are all you need for many projects. Once you are hooked, you will find that there are several tools available that can make a particular job easier or faster. But in the beginning, what you already have on hand will be more than enough to create objects you will be proud to display or give as gifts to family and friends.

Another wonderful aspect of crafting with gourds is how adaptable they are to any talent or skill you may already possess. The potter is thrilled to have a bowl,

platter, or lidded container already formed, just waiting for the addition of a design. The wood carver is presented with an already turned vessel that can be carved or shaped using many hand and power tools. The weaver has a round framework that can support off-loom weaving techniques. The basketmaker will find that the gourd provides an

Many years ago while visiting a friend, my attention was caught by a lovely "wooden" bowl on the shelf. When I asked her about it, she revealed that the bowl was a gourd she had found at a flower mart and brought home to embellish. She had cut off the top of the gourd and cleaned it; then she had rubbed on shoe polish and covered the rough edges with vines from the garden. In no time at all, she had created an object that was beautiful to look at and useful, too. This craft really captured my interest. With tools and supplies I already had in the kitchen or garage, I began to explore a whole new medium.

Many people who like to work with their hands are like me—fascinated with new crafts and new materials, and always willing to learn a new skill or find another way to explore artistic ideas. Unfortunately, this curiosity usually spawns a house and garage cluttered with fancy equipment, as well as numerous special tools and materials that continue to take up space long after the dream or inspiration has faded. Or perhaps the craft that looks and sounds so easy turns out to be more challenging

Gourds come in many shapes and sizes that can suggest projects or designs. Ginger Summit, *Painted Pheasant* and handled basket, photos by Sandra Stambaugh

ideal base for many basketry techniques. And with a simple preparatory base coat, the painter now has a round canvas on which to explore a new level of creativity.

But gourds are not just for the accomplished artist or craftsperson. They offer budding artists of all ages, including children, an easy-to-work-with medium that can be embellished quickly and easily. There is no "right or wrong" way to work with a gourd. Everyday materials and tools that are simple to master inspire confidence, filling the beginner with pride and lots of ideas for next projects. I love to teach gourd classes; the thrill of discovery brings out creative possibilities that many beginners have never experienced. The classes are simply fun, too; because all gourds are different, there is never any pressure to copy or reproduce another person's ideas. And because gourds are versatile, a mistake can quickly be turned into an asset with a new design or embellishment.

Most of the projects in this book have been planned to be both beautiful and functional. By changing the colors used, and adapting the designs to different shaped gourds, you can create art that will be welcome in any home, and be useful in many ways.

Gourds have been used for thousands of years by people all over the world as utensils, dishes, containers, storage vessels, and even simple musical instruments. Originally gourds most often were left undecorated and were simply taken for granted in all facets of daily life, much as we use plastic or metal tools and containers in our lives today. But in many cultures, gourds were embell-

ished with materials, designs, or patterns that ornamented other objects in that culture, such as weaving, woodcarving, burning and staining, etching or inlay. Beautiful examples of this work can be found in museums around the world.

Today artists continually draw inspiration from these examples. Historically, gourds have been an integral part of human cultural development, but were largely eclipsed by other materials, such as ceramics and metal. Thank goodness they are now being rediscovered and appreciated by artists, crafters, musicians, gardeners, and decorators. By re-creating the projects in this book you will be sharing the pleasures our human ancestors enjoyed when they decorated the humble gourd.

Top right: Dyan Mai Peterson, painted gourd basket with stick handle, photo by Tim Barnwell; center: Judy M. Mallow, painted gourd basket with pine needle rim and lid, photo by McKenzie Photography; bottom right: Linda Arias, *Dream Gourd*, canteen gourd with black background, photo by Richard Hasselberg

WHAT IS A GOURD?

Gourd Basics

Gourds come in a great variety of shapes and sizes. What's more, sometimes vegetables are labeled gourds when that is not what they are at all. So the first question to be answered is: What is a gourd?

Gourds are members of one of the largest botanical families, the Cucurbitaceae family, which also contains all melons and squash. Although many members of the Cucurbitaceae family are called gourds, especially in the fall, only three kinds dry with a hard shell—a fact that distinguishes a gourd from a squash.

the thin shell can be cracked and peeled to reveal a strong fibrous interior that has many uses, primarily as a scrubber in kitchen or bath. Luffas are often cut apart and used for a wide variety of crafts, but their principle use is for cleaning up.

■ The first is *Cucurbita pepo v. ovifera,* more commonly known as the *ornamental* gourd. These are seen in the markets in the fall in a beautiful array of shapes, sizes, and colors. They are often sold polished or varnished, which gives them a lovely sheen, but the finish clogs the pores of the shell so that the moisture inside remains trapped, causing the fruit to rot after several weeks. If left in a natural state, ornamental gourds will eventually dry with a firm thin shell and a fibrous pulp. These gourds make wonderful ornaments and holiday decorations, but because of their thin shell they are not often used for other craft purposes.

■ By far the most popular gourd for crafters is the *Lagenaria siceraria* or *hardshell* variety. These gourds have been used by people around the world for thousands of years for many purposes. Because of wide geographic distribution and use for many different tasks, hardshell gourds have hybridized to encompass a bewildering array of sizes and shapes. They can be grown throughout the United States, and seeds are readily available in catalogs, nurseries, and garden centers. For crafters who do not want to begin with a seed, dried gourds are available from gourd farms, specialty markets such as flower marts, and many farmers' markets.

■ The *luffa sponge gourd* looks much like a large cucumber or zucchini when growing, and is highly prized as a vegetable in India and the Far East. If allowed to dry,

PREPARING THE GOURD FOR CRAFTING

THE DRYING PROCESS

Gourds are edible while young, but when mature they have a thick shell and a tough, stringy interior. After many months, the moisture inside will evaporate to produce a firm woody shell that is filled with dried pulp and seeds. Most gourds available for crafters have already been dried and may be covered with a moldy, dirty exterior. This is the waxy epidermis or outer layer that protected the gourd as it was growing but was sloughed off as the moisture inside evaporated. When the gourd is completely dry,

the seeds may rattle when shaken or the pulp may thud against the interior.

Sometimes it's difficult to tell when the gourd is completely dry, but after working with a few gourds you will develop a feel for the weight and texture of a completely dry shell. The surface of the gourd shell is tan with a mottled pattern created by the drying epidermis.

Inspecting the Gourd

Carefully inspect the gourd shell. Just like all fruits and vegetables, gourds of a single variety, even those from the same vine, come in many shapes and sizes depending on soil, weather, and growing conditions. Look for blemishes, insect holes, and irregularities; these are not cause to discard the gourd—you may able to incorporate these marks in your design. Shells will vary in thickness and density, ranging from very thin shells $\frac{1}{4}$ inch (.6 cm) to almost 1 inch (2.5 cm) thick. It's often difficult to predict the thickness of a shell before it has been cut.

CLEANING THE GOURD

For all the projects in this book, and for all gourd crafting, you will need to clean the gourd shell to remove mold and dirt.

Gourd Cleaning Supplies

Basin with water

Metal kitchen scrub pad, scrub brush, or wire brush

Fine-grade sandpaper

First soak the gourd in warm water for up to 15 minutes, and then scrub off the mold and dirt with a metal kitchen scrub pad. For several projects in this book, the gourd is now ready to be painted or decorated. Some crafters prefer to go over the shell with very fine wet/dry sandpaper to remove any blemish or rough spot, but this step is optional.

Cutting the Gourd Shell to Clean the Interior

For most of the projects in this book, you will need to cut the gourd open and remove the seeds and pulp. Because the gourd is a soft woody sphere, most tools designed for woodworking are highly suitable for gourd craft as well. A complete list of cutting supplies and tools appears on page 14.

SAFETY CONCERNS

Many people are allergic to the dust created when cutting and cleaning the gourd. As a precaution, wear a mask during this portion of the work. Although some gourd crafters prefer to cut open the gourd outdoors, it is fine to do this step indoors, as long as the room is well ventilated. Also, you will eliminate most of the gourd dust if you soak or squirt the interior with water.

CUTTING THE GOURD

1 First select a gourd that is appropriate for your project, and mark a line where you will be cutting. One easy way to draw a line that will result in an evenly cut gourd is to steady your drawing hand on an object, such as a brick or book that is the right height for where you want to cut. Set the pencil point on the gourd and rotate the gourd as you draw the line.

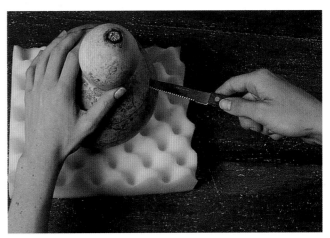

2 Stabilize the gourd on the foam pad. Use a sharp kitchen knife to make a hole in the gourd shell large enough to accommodate the blade of the small keyhole or hobby saw.

3 Use the saw to carefully cut around the line you have drawn on the gourd shell. You can also hold the gourd on your lap or between your knees as you saw it open. If you choose to work in this position, be sure to use a foam pad or a heavy apron to prevent the gourd from slipping.

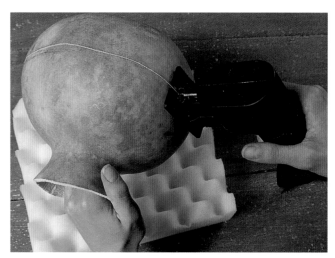

4 Remove the top, and then pull out all the loose pulp and seeds. Scrape out the pulp that is stuck on the interior shell with a serrated utensil, such as a grapefruit spoon. Many gourd crafters have favorite tools for this task, including sharp seashells, old kitchen spoons, and bent hacksaw blades (with the two ends wrapped together with many layers of tape). Search your kitchen or garage for a tool that works for you.

5 When the gourd interior is clean, file and sand the cut edge of the opening.

CUTTING A GOURD WITH A POWER SAW

You can also use a power saw to cut open a gourd. Many of the power jigsaws designed for use on wood are too heavy or too powerful for use on a fragile gourd shell. The weight of the saw and the rough reciprocal action of the blade tend to crack or chip the shell, rather than leave a nice, even cut. However there are several small jigsaws specifically designed for hobby crafters. The blades on these machines are thin, and the machine is very lightweight, allowing for flexible movement around the shell of the gourd, and leaving a clean, smooth edge.

To use this type of motorized saw, first make a hole in the gourd with a knife. With the motor off, insert the blade into the hole. Press the foot of the power tool firmly against the gourd shell and turn on the motor. Guide the saw along the lines drawn on the shell, all the while pressing the footplate against the gourd. When the cut is finished, turn off the motor *before* lifting the saw. (If you try to turn the motor on and off without the footplate pressed against the shell, the reciprocal movement of the blade may crack or mar the gourd surface.)

A word of caution: Rotary hobby power tools often come with a round saw blade about the size of a small coin. When attached to the tool handle, it spins much like a tiny circular saw. Designed for use on wood or other flat surfaces, this blade is not at all suitable for use on a gourd. The surface of the gourd is round and often slightly irregular, which causes the saw blade to bind or stall. This can be quite dangerous when you are working on a small gourd.

Cleaning Challenges

Occasionally some spots of pulp stubbornly remain stuck to the inside of the gourd. You can easily remove these by filling the gourd with water and letting the pulp soak for a while, even overnight if necessary. Then pour out the water, and use your scraping tools again.

Sometimes a gourd will be very smelly when it is cut open. Even after the seeds and pulp are removed, the shell will have a strong, unpleasant odor that may be difficult to get rid of. Possible remedies include:

1. Fill the gourd with baking soda—either dry, in a dilute water solution, or as a thick paste applied to the interior surface—and leave it there for several days. Then rinse and test the gourd. If the smell remains, repeat the process.

2. Fill the shell with water and then pour it out. Coat the interior liberally with borax soap. Leave it there for up to two days, and then brush out the dried borax (compliments of JoAnnis Mohrman).

3. Once the offensive odor is gone, fill the shell with a potpourri or with cotton swabs soaked in aromatic oils.

Repairing a Broken Gourd

Sometimes a gourd cracks when you cut it open or as you are decorating it with other cutting or carving techniques.

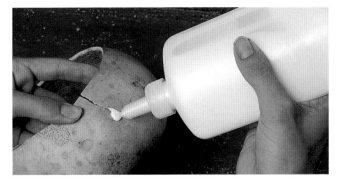

1 To repair a crack, apply a small amount of carpenter's glue.

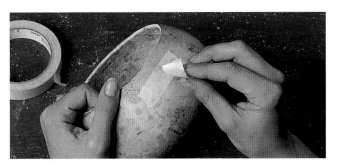

2 Tape the crack, and let the gourd dry overnight. Lightly sand the repair. For a larger hole or repair, make a bandage of gauze or silk that has been soaked in white glue. (I frequently use this technique on the inside of the gourd, and then cover the entire surface with decoupage or texture paint (see Pedestal Bowl with Decoupage Interior on page 57). Once the glue is thoroughly dry, fill in the edges and any rough surface with wood putty. Allow the area to dry overnight, and then sand smooth. A base coat of paint will cover the repair.

A crack or hole can also be stitched or laced. Many prized gourd containers from Africa have a row of lacing along an edge or a side, evidence of a valued utensil that has been repaired by pitch and stitching with cotton or vine. Contemporary crafters occasionally incorporate the laced mend of an accidental crack into an overall design.

Repairing a Natural Imperfection

Some gourd shells have pockmarks, holes, or other irregularities caused by insects or damage to the shell as it was growing. If you have a gourd like that, first make sure no live insects are trapped inside the shell. Then fill small holes, dents, or cracks with wood putty. This product is now available in many shades of tan and brown, so it's quite possible to find a shade that matches the shell. Once you have sanded this area, you can coat it with a light shoe polish, and the repair will be invisible. Some gourd crafters make a putty of white glue and gourd dust, which also blends into the shell.

Using Scraps

Because there are so many uses for gourd scraps, it's a good idea to save the gourd top you cut off when opening a gourd. Scraps come in handy when you want to practice a technique, such as carving or woodburning, or when you want to try out new surface decoration products. Some paints, leather dyes, and stains respond quite differently on a gourd shell than on canvas or paper, so it makes sense to test the materials first on a gourd scrap before applying them to your potential work of art.

Gourd scraps can be used to make jewelry and hair accessories, too. In addition, small pieces can be joined to other gourds to create bases, handles—even beaks and ears for animal figures (see Mother Goose Birdhouse, page 39).

Gourd Cutting Supplies and Tools

SAWS:

Keyhole saw

Hand hobby saw

Craft knife

Power saw

Kitchen knife

SCRAPERS:

Serrated grapefruit spoon

Leather hide scraper

Clay shapers

Bent hacksaw blades

Shell

FILES:

Flat

Riffler

SANDPAPER:

Variety of grades

DRILLS:

Multiple size bits for holes

Hole bit

HAND-HELD MOTORIZED CUTTING TOOL:

Sanding and carving bits

GLOVES:

Garden gloves

Fish fileting or supple leather gloves (for working with gouges)

OTHER SUPPLIES:

Carpenter's glue

Masking tape

Wood putty

Foam pad (to stabilize gourd on work surface)

Pencil or chalk

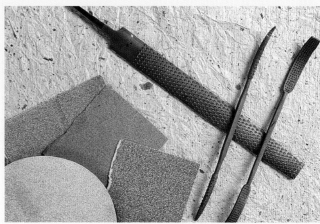

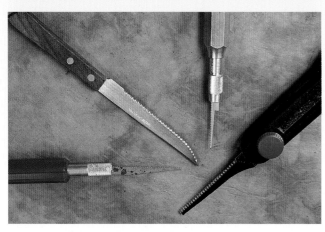

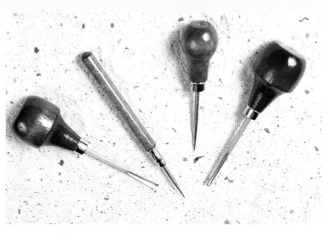

Top left: taxidermy scraping tool, hacksaw blade, oyster shell, grapefruit spoon, butter curler; top right: wood rasp, riffler files, sandpaper, palm sander; bottom right: wood gouges, leather awls; bottom left: kitchen knife, hobby saws, keyhole saw

PREPARING THE GOURD SHELL

Gourd shells are extremely varied in surface, texture, and porosity. Even within a single shell there are areas that may be slick and smooth, and other areas that are softer or more porous. Coloring and finishing products that are used with paper, leather, and wool are all suitable for use on a gourd shell, but may have very unpredictable results. Colors may have different hues or intensities; dyes, inks, and stains may penetrate one area and have little noticeable effect on others. If you are flexible and willing to adapt your project to the nuances of the gourd, you will enjoy constant challenges and unexpected joys in your gourd adventures.

Gourd shells can be sanded lightly with fine wet/dry sandpaper, or rubbed with steel wool before beginning a project. This will help to provide "tooth" for paints to bond to the shell and will even out the surface of the gourd, allowing colors to penetrate the shell more consistently.

However, do not use coarse sandpaper for this purpose: the grooves created by rough sanding will be dramatically exaggerated by stains or dyes.

COLORING THE GOURD

While all coloring media are suitable and have been used to embellish gourds, it's important to keep in mind the differences in types of products as you make your selection.

Color Pigments

Paint pigments, such as oil paints, acrylic, tempera, water colors, oil pastels, etc., all contain color pigments that are bonded by an agent (i.e. oil, wax, acrylic, etc.). When applied to a surface such as canvas, paper, or a gourd shell, the agent dries and the pigment remains adhered to the surface. If you make a mistake in your design on the gourd shell, it's

usually easy to correct by simply cleaning off the pigment with water or paint remover as recommended by the manufacturer.

When using paints, it's a good idea to seal the surface first with a light spray of clear varnish or a base coat of paint. This will provide a smooth surface that will be much easier to paint on.

Once the paints are completely dry, they must be protected, either by varnish or polyurethene, so they do not chip, peel, or otherwise flake off the surface.

Stains, Inks, and Dyes

Stains, inks, and dyes are designed to penetrate the surface on which they are applied. Usually once these are applied on a gourd, the shell is permanently colored. While some dyes may respond to a bleaching agent, most colors cannot be removed completely. Most gourd shells have a somewhat mottled pattern as a result of the curing process, and these patterns will be emphasized by the stains or dyes. Softer portions of the shell will absorb more of the stains and appear darker than other areas. Soft inner shells that are exposed by carving, or the interior of the

gourd, will also absorb more of the stain and will appear much darker than the smooth outer shell surface.

Stains are readily available in hardware and home-improvement stores in a broad variety of wood-tone hues, all of which are very compatible with the gourd shell. Dyes are available for many different functions, but the

ones intended for leather are the most compatible with the gourd shell and come in a wide variety of rich colors. These dyes are available from leather stores, shoe repairs shops, and some shoe stores. Inks can be painted on with a brush or dauber, or applied with a pen. Both water-based and permanent marking pens are suitable for gourd craft. The variety of colors and tips available in marking pens make them a popular choice for beginning crafters.

Wax and Cream Shoe Polish

Another product that is very successful on gourd shells is wax or cream shoe polish. These leather polishes and waxes now are available in an exciting array of colors and finishes. A light coat of colored wax can provide a subtle sheen or luster to the gourd shell. For more intense color, apply several coats of the same or different colors. By leaving the wax on the shell for a while before buffing, the colors will have a chance to penetrate the shell. I frequently set a gourd shell that has been heavily waxed out in the hot summer sun or in a warm oven. The wax melts and the pigments penetrate the shell. Allow the gourd to cool before buffing, and you will be rewarded with a rich, soft leatherlike surface.

Treating the Interior Surface

One of the surfaces often neglected is the interior of the gourd. Consider finishing this surface once it's thoroughly cleaned, particularly if it's discolored by black or mottled patterns. Many gourd artists spray the surface with black or dark spray paint. Acrylic or latex paint may also be used. Textured paints now available in many craft

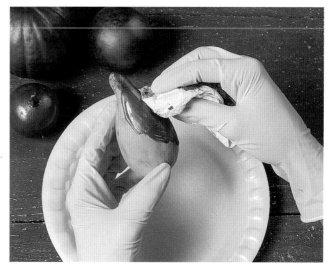

stores provide a new and interesting contrast to the traditional gourd interiors (see Simple Candleholders, page 34). Decoupage is another attractive approach, as the photograph below illustrates.

Whatever product you choose for your gourd project can be applied with any tool or technique with which you are comfortable. Brushes, sponges, daubers, a soft cloth or paper towel are all good choices. If you have never worked with gourds, you don't need to rush out to buy expensive tools and equipment. Once you discover a technique that you want to pursue, you may want to buy specialized tools. But when beginning, just use what is already in your kitchen, garage, or hobby corner. Because gourds can be used with so many embellishment techniques, there is no limit to the tools that can be used by the crafter.

Woodburning

Many of the projects in this book include woodburning as a decorative technique. Darkening the shell by applying heat is a technique that has been used for thousands of years. Native Americans and artists in West Africa heated spears or pounded metal to press against or sear designs in gourd containers. Artists in Peru blow on burning eucalyptus sticks to scorch patterns in the shell.

Fortunately there are several simple tools readily available in craft and hardware stores that work very well in gourd craft. Most of these tools have a variety of interchangeable tips, each of which is designed to produce a different type of line, mark, or impression on the surface. Experiment with the tips that come with the woodburning tool to find which works best for your style of design. Also, some brands of woodburning tool come in different watts, which indicate the intensity of heat produced. Be sure to select the instrument that has the most wattage, since gourd shells are very dense and require

intense heat for successful crafting. Practice holding the woodburning tool in many positions to find the one that works for you. Because the tip is a relatively long distance from the hand, many people brace their wrist or baby finger against the gourd shell to stabilize the tool. Hands and tools all come in different sizes, so practice with many positions as you explore the use of this versatile tool.

tious of the possibility of fire: a bucket of water nearby is a good idea when burning wood, even with a simple woodburning tool.

Carving

Because the gourd shell is basically a soft wooden container, all tools used for woodcarving are equally suitable for use on the gourd. There are many carving techniques, and in this book, we use two different styles. Books on carving may suggest other techniques you may want to explore. I strongly suggest that you practice on gourd scraps to find the most successful combination of tool and technique.

By using a variety of sizes of drill bits, it's possible to create a lacy effect of multiple openings in a gourd shell. Some of these openings can be further shaped by hobby knives or files to create interesting designs. A small hobby saw, either hand or power, can be used to create intricate patterns for candle surrounds or lamp shades.

In addition to the more conventional woodburning tool, one project (Scorched Tea Cups, page 46) introduces a new way to use a simple soldering tool. The concentrated flame of this handy butane torch is just right to reproduce primitive scorched designs. Experiment on gourd scraps to explore the different effects this tool can produce and the many ways it can be combined with other techniques and tools to create unusual designs.

If the smell of the burning gourd shell bothers you, wear a respirator mask. Some artists even wear goggles to keep the fumes from the eyes. I always woodburn in a well-ventilated area, preferably outdoors. I am also cau-

Surface designs can be carved in the shell, taking advantage of the lighter inner shell to provide texture and color contrast. There are many ways the qualities of inner and outer shell can be emphasized. By dyeing the outer shell prior to carving, the pale interior provides a dramatic background for the design (Relief Carved Bowl, page 62). If you dye or stain the project after it has been carved, the softer inner surface will absorb more of the coloration and appear much darker than the smooth exterior (Carved Vase, page 60).

Both hand and power hobby tools are suitable for carving designs in the shell. When doing surface carving, try to select a gourd with a thick shell. This is not always easy to tell, especially when you are just beginning gourd craft. With more experience you will be able to tell by weight or by tapping the shell which gourds have shells that are thicker than others of similar size.

If you use hand gouges, make sure that the tools are always sharp. Dull cutting edges tend to produce ragged edges and rough cuts. Always wear a protective glove on the hand holding the shell, since the round shell is frequently slippery for a beginning carver.

Hobby power tools are a very popular choice for gourd carving. Many different size bits are readily available for these tools, and projects that may be difficult with hand tools are relatively fast and simple with these motorized tools. Some of these hand-held power tools may be somewhat heavy, particularly after you have been holding them for a while. Experiment with ways to brace or support your hand or arm so that the weight of the tool does not distort your design. In addition to carving, the bits available for these tools can be adapted to help with such tasks as sanding, filing, or shaping edges, and even with cleaning the inside of small gourds.

A word of caution: Motorized hand-held hobby tools produce a great deal of dust as well as noise. Protect your ears with rubber earplugs, and wear a mask and goggles. I always try to use this tool outdoors to eliminate mess in the house.

PROTECTIVE FINISHES

There are many options for finishing a gourd shell so that it, and your art, will be preserved for years to come. The options for finishing a gourd include all waxes and polishes intended for floors, furniture, shoes and leather, as well as different varnishes, shellac, polyurethane, wood sealers, wood stains, and even resin.

When selecting a wax, first decide if you prefer one with a coloring or a tint, or one that is perfectly clear. Most floor waxes are designed to dry hard and clear, leaving a deep luster when buffed. Furniture polishes often include a "scratch remover" which is actually a stain that penetrates the wood, or, in this case, the gourd shell. This subtle addition of stain can greatly enhance the texture of the gourd shell, and is often highly desirable. Liquid furniture polish adds a subtle luster and does not require rubbing or buffing. Take care in applying a wax over a painted surface; the mild abrasive in waxes will wipe off many paints and even alter some dyes.

Varnishes and other similar protective coatings are available in both spray cans or for applying with a brush. If your choice for embellishment has included paints or dyes, be sure to read and follow the manufacturer's recommendations before applying a protective coating. Solvents or chemicals that are in the paints or dyes will react with those in the finishing product; many beautiful works of art have been accidentally ruined by a spray finish that caused a paint, ink, or dye to run or bleed.

It's a good idea to use gourd scraps to test combinations of coloring products and finishes. Label these experiments, even the ones that don't work, for future reference. *Tip:* If there is any possibility that the design will be affected by the chemicals in a protective finish, I will spray on an initial very light coat, allow it to dry, and then apply more coats, taking care each time that the paint, stain, or dye is not affected.

Protecting the Gourd from Nature's Elements

Many of the materials used to color the gourd shell will fade in sunlight over time. This is particularly true of dyes, stains, and inks. Varnishes that contain ultraviolet light shields may offer some protection, but the best precaution is to keep the art out of direct sun, if possible.

By their very nature, gourds are biodegradable. Gourds left outside will eventually respond to the elements—they may discolor, absorb moisture, and then soften, bleach, and generally weaken. For birdhouses, bird feeders, and other gourd crafts that are intended for outdoor use, soak the gourd in a light wood preservative for protection before you cut or decorate the gourd. (A light application will not be harmful for nestlings.) Two or more coats of exterior varnish or paint will also help seal and protect the surface for a season of use.

However, by far the greatest threat to gourds is from living creatures—rodents, such as mice and squirrels, and any number of insects. Gourds make wonderful homes, not only for birds, but for many other living things, too. I have had many birdhouses turned into lacy mobiles by creative squirrels.

If you suspect insects have moved into the interior of a gourd that is already decorated or embellished, there are several options you can try. If the gourd is small (and thoroughly dry), put it in the microwave oven for a couple of minutes. A larger gourd can be sealed in a plastic bag and put in the freezer for up to a week. Unfortunately, this may not kill some insects—they may simply assume it's winter and go into a dormant state. A third option is to put the gourd into a plastic bag and add a rag soaked in insecticide. Some gourd crafters suggest using mothballs to discourage bugs from moving in. With any luck, one of these methods will eliminate the bug invasion without harming the embellishment on the shell.

Finishes for the Gourd Interior for Use with Food

The interior of a gourd shell does not need finishing, other than thorough cleaning, even when the gourd is used to hold food or drinking water. Bowls, cups, canteens, pitchers, and other utensils used for food should be soaked in

water to which 1 to 3 tablespoons of baking soda has been added to remove any bitter taste. After several days, empty, rinse, and then taste the water. If a bitter taste remains, repeat the process until the flavor of the water is clean. Traditionally, gourds designed to hold food were not sealed in any way. Moisture that leaches through the shell evaporates and cools the container, which is why for centuries gourd canteens have been used to carry drinking water.

If you prefer, the interior can be sealed with other products, including melted paraffin, butcher block and salad bowl finish, and polyurethane. *Safety Note:* When finishing a gourd to be used with food, never substitute varnish for polyurethane, because the varnish will remain toxic when it dries. Once polyurethane products are completely dry, the surface is nontoxic and safe for use with food. Check the label on the container before you purchase a product; if it's recommended for use on children's toys or for objects in the kitchen, such as butcher block surfaces, then it's safe for gourd containers that will hold food.

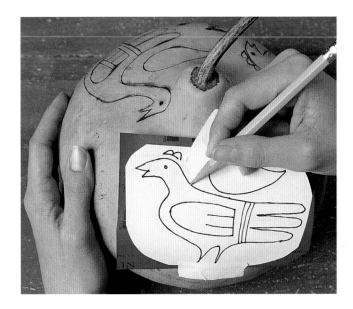

Transferring a Design onto the Gourd

There are two simple ways to transfer a design onto the gourd shell.

■ Carbon Paper: If you're trying to copy an image or pattern, first enlarge it on a copier to the size indicated. Position the copy over a piece of carbon paper in the correct area on the gourd; then lightly trace over the lines with a pencil. When you're finished, the design will be lightly sketched on the gourd. If you don't have any carbon paper, you can make your own; enlarge the pattern, turn the paper over and thoroughly pencil over the back of the paper. Place the paper, pencil-colored side down, on the gourd, and trace over the pattern. The graphite from the pencil will work like carbon paper.

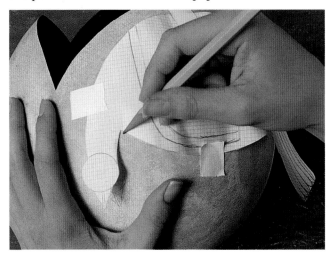

■ Paper Template: You can also transfer a design by creating a paper template. First enlarge the drawing on a copier to the size indicated. Cut it out, tape it to the gourd, and trace around it.

Linda Arias, *Virgin of Guadalupe*, large and small painted gourds, photo by Richard Hasselberg

Simple Fruits and Vegetables

Grace your table with an array of ornamental gourds colored to look like fruits and vegetables. Their shape will suggest which food they can imitate. These gourds are also very attractive as accents on a wreath. Equipped with a hanger, they make lovely Christmas tree ornaments as well.

YOU WILL NEED

Assortment of dried ornamental gourds

Gourd cleaning supplies

Leather dyes or acrylic paints

Paintbrush

Rubber or latex gloves

Paper towel or soft rag

Metallic paint pens (optional)

To add stems or hangers:

Small gourd stems

Drill

Thin gold cord

Craft glue

1 Select ornamental gourds of many different shapes, sizes, and surface textures. Clean the outside of the gourds.

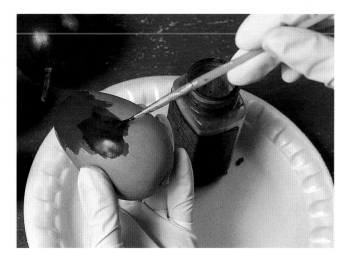

2 With your hands protected by plastic gloves, brush or wipe on leather dye.

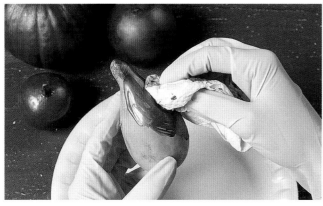

3 To achieve a translucent effect with paint, wipe on thinned paint and then, while it is still wet, wipe it off. You can use several shades of colors to create a more realistic fruit or vegetable appearance. Let the leather dye or paint dry.

4 To increase the lifelike effect, you can also add leaves and stems (gourd stems often fall off). First drill a small hole in the stem end of the gourd.

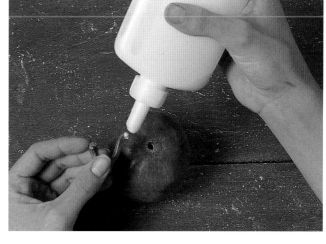

5 Then glue a new stem in place, and allow it to dry. Leaves can be cut from scraps of gourd shell and then colored with leather dyes.

6 To make ornaments, embellish the painted gourds with metallic paint pens, and let dry.

7 Drill a hole in the stem end of the gourd as described in step 4. Then glue in a loop of gold cord. You can hide the hole, if necessary, with a bead or a jewelry finding.

Flowerpots with Upholstery Tacks

These flowerpots are easy to make and can be colored to complement your home decor. The sheen on the small gourd was created by applying gold shoe polish on top of a dry coat of black shoe polish. Even though the interior of the gourd is sealed, be sure to set a plastic saucer in the bottom of the bowl to catch drips from the potted plant. The brass feet allow plenty of air circulation under the pot, so moisture won't harm your tabletop.

YOU WILL NEED

Gourd

Gourd cleaning supplies

Small saw

Files and sandpaper

Shoe polish

Rubber or latex gloves

Paper towel or soft rag

Awl

Upholstery tacks

Pliers

Paraffin

Double boiler set up

Paintbrush

Gardening gloves

Bristle brush

Screw-on brass knobs

Plastic saucer

Potted plant

1 Clean the outside of the gourd. Stabilize the gourd on the foam pad and cut off the top. Remove the seeds and pulp. File and sand the cut edge. Wipe shoe polish on the exterior surface of the gourd, wearing gloves to protect your hands.

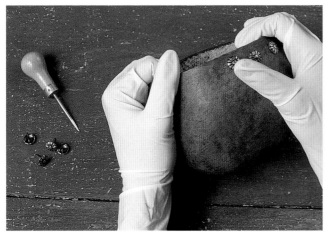

2 Push the tacks into the gourd, spacing them about ½ to 1 inch (1.3 to 2.5 cm) apart. If the gourd has a particularly thick shell, use the awl to punch holes first.

3 Use pliers to pinch the sharp points of the tacks against the inner surface of the gourd.

4 Brush the gourd surface to bring out the sheen of the leather polish.

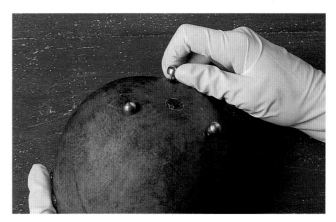

5 Screw three small brass knobs through the bottom of the gourd to stabilize it.

6 Heat the paraffin in a double boiler (take care not to overheat: melted wax is highly flammable.) While the wax is melting, heat the gourd in a 200°F (93°C) oven. Hold the warm gourd in a gloved hand, and brush the melted wax onto the interior of the gourd. Let dry. Tip: It is important to apply the wax to a warm gourd so that it will penetrate the shell; wax applied to a cool shell will peel off.

Southwest-Style Mask

Masks were used by most early cultures in ceremonies and dances to summon the benevolent spirits. Be a part of this ancient tradition by creating a great-looking mask to decorate your home. Masks can be simple or ornate, fanciful or lifelike. Different shapes of gourds will suggest the style of ornamentation that will bring out each gourd's true spirit.

YOU WILL NEED

Round gourd

Gourd cleaning supplies

Pencil or chalk

Small saw

Files and sandpaper

Wood glue

Artist-quality wax crayons*

Cotton swabs

Art gum eraser

Red and black permanent markers

Waxed linen

Assorted beads

Feathers

Awl

*Artist crayons are available in most art- and craft-supply stores, and come in a range of colors. Do not use children's crayons; they will not give the same results.

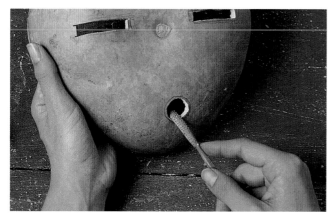

1 Clean the outside of the gourd. Mark on the gourd where you will cut the piece that will become the mask; then use the saw to cut it off. Clean the cut piece, and file and sand the edges. Mark the location of the eyes and mouth. Use a handsaw or a power saw to cut the slits for the eyes. Cut a section from a dipper gourd to use as the mouth plug. Use a drill to cut the mouth, and then enlarge the hole with a file.

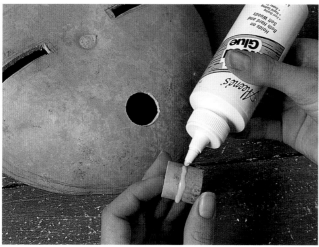

2 Glue in the mouth plug and let dry.

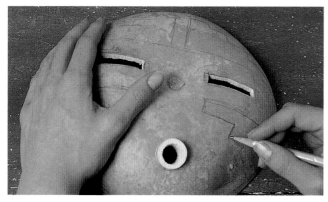

3 Using the photograph on page 26 as a guide, sketch on the facial designs.

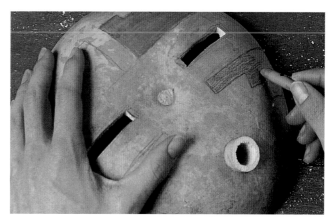

4 Color in the designs with wax crayons. You can add several colors to create a shaded or blended effect. Apply more than one "coat" to darken the color.

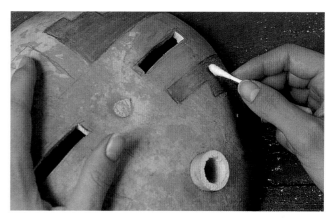

5 Use the cotton swabs to blend and smooth the crayons. Erase any pencil lines. Color the inside of the eyes and mouth with markers.

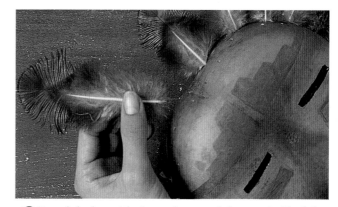

6 Punch holes with the awl around the top half of the mask perimeter. Add a drop of glue to the end of each feather and push it into a hole. Cut two pieces of waxed linen, each about 3 inches (8 cm) long. String each piece with a few beads, leaving a long tail. Make a hole on each side of the mask where you want the earrings to go. Slip the linen tail through the hole and tie the end with a large knot.

Mexican Painted Dippers

For thousands of years around the world, gourd dippers have been used as cups or spoons, usually undecorated, with a clean but unfinished interior. To make a dipper gourd that will add a festive touch to your kitchen, paint the outside with the brilliant colors and designs of Mexico. Even if you don't drink from it, the dipper will remind you of the ancient beginnings of gourds in the home.

YOU WILL NEED

Dipper gourd

Gourd cleaning supplies

Pencil

Foam pad

Small saw

Files and sandpaper

Salad bowl oil*

Paintbrush

Acrylic paints in primary colors

Artist's paintbrush

Fine-tip black paint pen or permanent marker

Dimensional paint

Clear polyurethane spray (optional)

Awl (optional)

Leather thong or ribbon (optional)

*This product seals and finishes wooden salad bowls, butcher block surfaces, and cutting boards. It is available in most hardware stores.

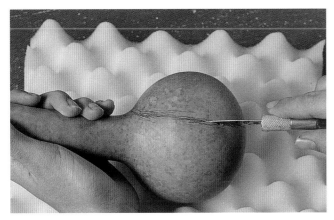

1 Clean the outside of the gourd. Draw a circle on the bulb area to indicate where to cut the opening. Stabilize the bulb end on the foam pad, and cut off the penciled area. Clean the interior. File and sand the cut edge.

2 Brush a coat of salad bowl oil on the interior of the dipper.

3 Copy (enlarge or reduce) the patterns on page 30 and transfer the design onto the outside of the dipper, or use your own imagination and sketch your own design. Be sure to include the handle in your design.

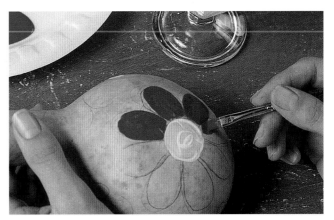

4 Use acrylic paints to fill in the design.

5 Add detail lines with the black paint pen or permanent marker. Let dry.

6 Use dimensional paints to create texture. Let dry. If you want, you can spray the exterior of the dipper with clear polyurethane. Tip: Be sure to test the spray on a scrap of gourd to make sure the finish will not cause the lines made by the marking pen to run.

Santa Claus Figure

Many bottle gourds have a Santa hiding inside, just waiting to be painted and added to your favorite holiday decorations. You can simplify or embellish the face, depending on your painting skill and artistic preference. To complete this kindly Saint Nick, be sure to add decoration to the robe, both front and back. By cutting off the bottom of the gourd and mounting it on a base, you can help Santa stand straight and tall.

YOU WILL NEED

Bottle gourd

Gourd cleaning supplies

Pencil

Small saw

File and sandpaper

Masking tape

Assorted paintbrushes, including fine-point

Plastic knife or craft stick

Acrylic paints: barn red, flesh, pink, burnt umber, white, blue, black, gray, forest green, kelly green, yellow

Santa face template

Carbon paper

Sponge

Textured white paint

Plywood or heavy cardboard, the same diameter as the bottom of the gourd

Piece of felt or leather (optional)

Wood glue

Clear spray varnis

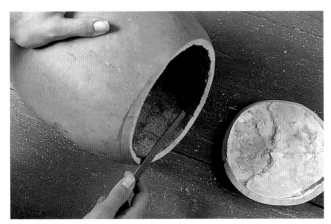

1 Select a bottle gourd that has a small top for the head and a larger base for the body. If the gourd doesn't stand straight, mark a circle around the bottom, and cut it off. Clean the gourd and remove the seeds and pulp. Lightly sand the surface of the gourd; this roughens the surface slightly and allows for a stronger bonding of the paint to the gourd.

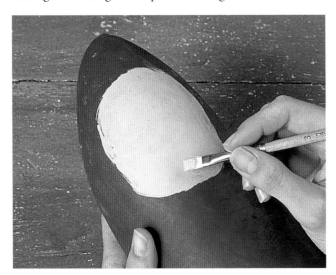

2 Paint the entire gourd barn red, and let dry. Use flesh-colored paint to cover the area of the face, and let dry.

3 Use a copier to reduce or expand the face template to make it the correct size for your gourd. Use carbon paper to transfer the drawing onto the flesh-colored area. Tip: If you don't have carbon paper, blacken the back of the template with a soft pencil. Then turn the paper over and trace the facial outline onto the gourd. The graphite will transfer to the gourd much like carbon paper.

4 Paint the facial details with flesh, pink, burnt umber, yellow, white, and blue paint. Add black for the eyebrows, mustache, and beard.

5 With white paint, add details to the eyebrows, mustache, and beard.

6 Use a sponge and black acrylic paint mixed with barn red to create shading for the arms, folds of the robe, and hood.

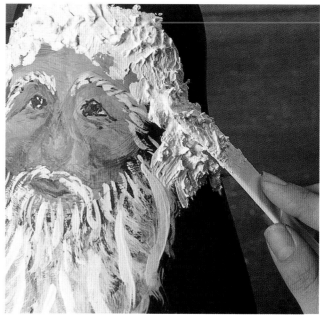

7 Use a plastic knife or craft stick to apply thick textured white paint for the fur of the hood, cuffs, and edge of the robe. Using the photograph on page 31 as a guide, add the other details, such as the holly wreath.

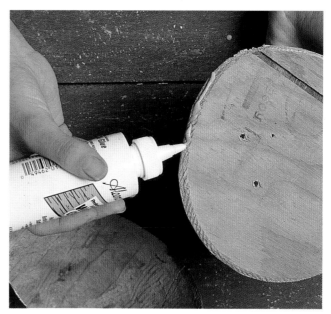

8 Set the gourd on a piece of plywood or thick cardboard, and trace around the bottom to mark a circle. Cut out the disk and sand or trim it so that it fits evenly inside the bottom of the gourd; then glue it in place. If you want, you can cover the outer surface of the base with leather or felt. Spray the entire gourd with varnish, and let dry.

Simple Candleholders

The more you work with gourds, the more inventive you will become about using the different parts to make a variety of items. Here, the center section of a bottle gourd has been transformed into a handsome candleholder, colored with shoe polish and accented with a leather thong and a brass bead. Because gourds come in so many different sizes and shapes, each candleholder will be unique.

YOU WILL NEED
Bottle gourd
Gourd cleaning supplies
Pencil
Foam pad
Small saw
File and sandpaper
Textured sandstone paint
Paintbrush
Shoe polish
Paper towel or soft rag
Stiff bristle brush
Leather thong
Brass bead

1 Clean the outside of the gourd. Mark where you plan to make your two cuts. Stabilize the gourd on the foam pad and cut off both the top and the bottom of the gourd, saving the center section for the candleholder. Clean the interior of the gourd. Use files and sandpaper to smooth and round the cut edges.

2 Paint the interior surface of the gourd using two coats of textured paint.

3 Color the exterior of the gourd with shoe polish, and let dry.

4 Buff the exterior of the gourd with the bristle brush.

5 Thread the brass bead onto the leather thong, and tie it around the waist of the gourd.

These eye-catching candleholders were wrapped with leather straps and cord, then decorated with beads. The white candlestick was colored with two coats of white shoe polish. The other was colored first with black shoe polish. Then silver polish was very lightly daubed on with a sponge to give a metallic finish.

Lidded Container with Painted Bird

The cut for the lid of this container is beautifully incorporated into the design, matching both the perfectly round basketball gourd and the ancient Mimbres pottery pattern. Gourds were one of the original containers used by the Indians in the Southwest, although gourds gradually were replaced by pottery and baskets. Today many of the designs that have been found on ancient pots and bowls are once again being used on gourds to provide beautiful reminders of our cultural heritage.

This stunning project was made by Janet Hatfield.

YOU WILL NEED

Basketball gourd

Gourd cleaning supplies

Pencil

Foam pad

Saw, with fine blade

Sandpaper

Rubber or latex gloves

White acrylic paint

Paper towels or soft rag

Black acrylic spray paint

Goose and ball templates

Scissors

Masking tape

Fine- and broad-tip black paint pens or permanent markers

1 Clean the outside of the gourd. Mark a triangle at the stem end of the gourd where you will cut out the lid. Stabilize the gourd on the foam pad and cut out the lid with a saw. Clean the interior thoroughly. Tip: To maintain a close fit between the lid and container, saw carefully with a fine saw blade, and sand as little as possible.

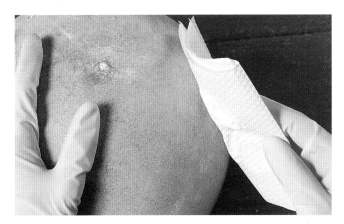

2 Thin a small amount of white paint and wipe it all over the gourd pot and lid. Before the paint dries, wipe most of it off so that you wind up with a pickled effect that allows the texture of the gourd to show.

3 Spray the interior of the gourd and the inside of the lid black, and let dry.

4 On a copier, enlarge the bird template to fit your gourd. Cut out the bird and tape it to the gourd. Trace around the shape. Remove the template.

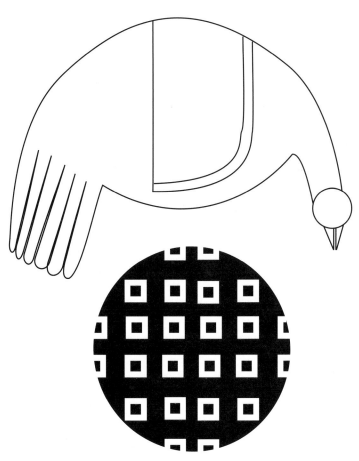

5 Use the fine-tip black permanent marker or paint pen to outline the body. Use the broad-tip marker or pen to fill in the larger areas.

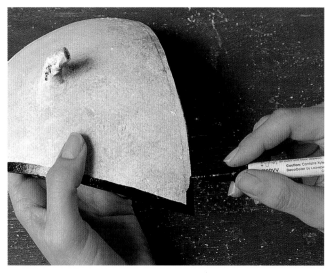

7 Paint a black border around the lid using a paint pen or marker.

6 Cut out the wing area on the template and tape it onto the gourd, over the outlined shape. Use the paint pen or marker to add the wing details. Enlarge the circle template on page 37 to fit the gourd. Cut it out and tape it to the gourd. Use it as a stencil to paint the circle, using the photograph with step 8 as a guide.

8 Once the design is completed on the pot and lid, lightly spray the outside of the gourd pieces with acrylic varnish to protect the surface. Let dry.

Mother Goose Birdhouse

Gourds make great birdhouses, a fact well known to our feathered friends around the world. The unmistakable shape of this gourd makes it the perfect choice for a bird habitat: what baby bird would not want to be protected by this kindly figure? Gourd birdhouses can be decorated in many different ways or left unadorned. A coat of white latex or acrylic paint will serve to reflect the heat and keep the interior of the house cooler in summer, and exterior varnish will prolong the life of the gourd.

YOU WILL NEED

Gourd with bent neck*

Gourd cleaning supplies

Stem of separate gourd

Foam pad

Small saw

File

Pencil

Small, motorized cutting tool (optional)

Wood glue

Wood putty (optional)

Drill with hole bit

Sandpaper

Acrylic paints: cream, brown, tan, gold, copper, black, turquoise

Soft cloth or paper towel

Sponge

Scissors

Clear, exterior varnish

Paintbrush

Leather scraps

2 pieces of sturdy wire, approximately 4 inches (5 cm) long each

Waxed linen

2 buttons, beads, or tacks

Awl

Leather cord

*Look for a gourd with a long neck between the small top bulb and the larger base.

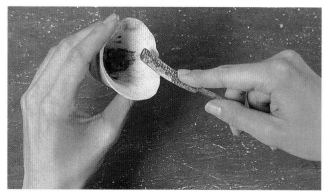

1 Clean the outside of the gourd. If you're lucky, you may find a gourd with a natural tapering point at the stem end to serve as the beak; more likely, you'll need to create one. Saw the stem end off another gourd with a diameter that will fit well on the stem end of the larger gourd. Clip the stem off the larger gourd. Use the file to smooth the edges until the new piece fits snugly against the stem end of the gourd shell.

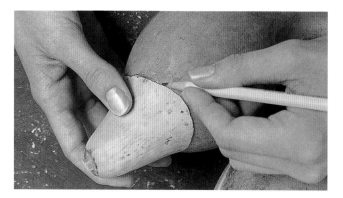

2 Hold the beak piece against the stem end of the gourd, and trace around it with the pencil.

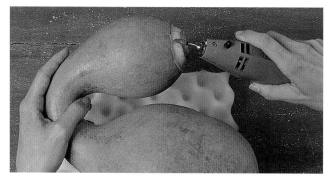

3 Following this line, use the small, motorized cutting tool to make a 1-inch-wide (2.5 cm) circular groove around the stem end of the gourd; this groove will be the base for the new beak. Shape and smooth the head of the larger gourd so that the beak conforms to the existing shape of the head.

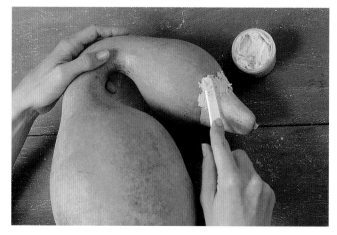

4 Attach the beak with wood glue; if necessary, smooth the joint with wood putty. Let dry overnight. Use a drill with a hole bit to make an entry hole in the body of the birdhouse. Make sure the hole is the appropriate size for the birds you are hoping to attract. Smooth the cut edges with sandpaper.

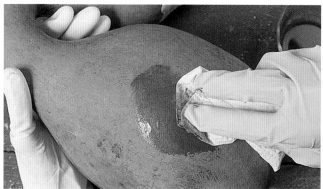

5 Dilute the cream-colored paint to make a wash the consistency of heavy cream; with a cloth or paper towel, rub it over the areas of the gourd that are the goose's belly, neck, and jaw. Make a wash with the brown paint and rub it on the gourd to color the goose's back, neck, head, and beak. Let these base coats dry. To add color and texture to the beak, rub on a wash of gold or tan paint, and let dry.

6 Cut the kitchen sponge into several u-shaped pieces of different sizes. Pour a small amount of copper, cream, turquoise, and black paint onto a plate. Dip a large sponge piece into one of the colors and stamp all over both sides of the gourd to create wing feathers. Repeat this process with another large sponge piece and the turquoise paint; then repeat with black paint. Use the smaller sponges and the cream and copper paints to add feathers to the belly and back. Once the paint has dried completely, apply at least two coats of exterior varnish to protect the gourd, and let dry.

8 Bind the leather snugly with the waxed linen. Bend the wire slightly to form a leg. Repeat these steps with the second piece of wire and leather to form the second leg. Drill two holes in the bottom of the bird, insert the legs, and attach them with wood glue. Let dry overnight.

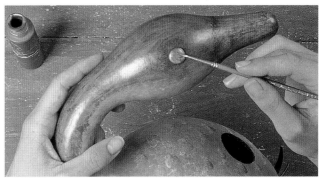

9 Use wood glue to attach beads, buttons, or tacks to create the eyes. The eyes shown here are clear, flat buttons painted turquoise blue.

7 To form the feet, cut three slits, each 1 to 1½ inches (2.5 to 3.8 cm) long, in the lower half of a 2-inch-wide (5 cm) piece of leather. Bend one of the wire pieces in half, and wrap the uncut portion of the leather around the wire, leaving the cut end to extend freely—these, of course, are the toes.

10 Use the awl to make five drainage holes in the bottom of the birdhouse. Then poke holes on either side of the gourd neck, and string a length of leather cord through the holes, and knot it securely.

GALLERY

Top left: Dyan Mai Peterson, painted gourds with sticks and beads, photo by Tim Barnwell; center: Eileen Marcotte, *Journey Within*, carved gourd mask with leather dye, acrylic paints, coco fiber hair, palm bark, and beads, photo by Richard Hasselberg; bottom right: Jerraldine Masten Hansen, painted gourd with nontoxic stencil paint, finished with nontoxic outdoor sealer; bottom left: Marguerite Smith, *Leaping Lizards*, wood-burning, carving, acrylic paints, leather dye, with inlaid turquoise, photo by Paul Smith

Tortilla Warmer

This lidded container can be used to protect many treasures, from jewelry to warm tortillas. Thousands of years ago Indians heated their foods by putting hot rocks in gourd bowls that held soups or stews. You can purchase a ceramic disk for this purpose or find a smooth rock; heat the disk or rock in the oven and set it in the container under a napkin. Your tortillas, biscuits, or rolls will stay warm throughout your meal under the gaze of these watchful hens.

YOU WILL NEED

Small birdhouse gourd with a broad base

Gourd cleaning supplies

Foam pad

Small saw

Files and sandpaper

Pencil

Template

Carbon paper

Masking tape

Woodburning tool

Oil pastels

Cotton swabs or stubbies

Manual flexible palm sander

Drill

Leather thong

Melted paraffin, polyurethane, or salad bowl oil

Paintbrush

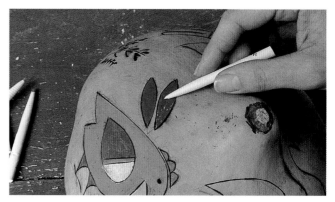

1 Clean the outside of the gourd. Enlarge the three bird templates (page 45) so they will fit on your gourd. Transfer the designs onto the gourd using carbon paper. Mark the line in the middle of the gourd where you will cut to create the lid, but do not cut now. Using the photograph on page 43 as a guide, sketch the flowers and leaves.

4 Use a cotton swab or stubbie to rub the pigment into the gourd shell. Once the pigments are firmly rubbed in, they are quite permanent. For additional protection, you can spray the outside of the gourd with polyurethane. Do not buff with wax, for the abrasive in the wax may remove the pigments.

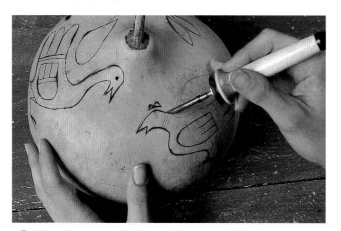

2 Woodburn the birds and the rest of the design onto the gourd. Stabilize the gourd on the foam pad, and cut off the lid. Thoroughly clean the interior, but do not sand the edges of the lid or it will not fit snugly on the pot.

5 To create a handle for the lid, drill a small hole in the stem end of the gourd. Thread a loop of leather through the hole, and tie the end on the inside of the lid.

3 Using the photograph as a guide, color in the birds, flowers, and leaves with the oil pastels.

6 Finish cleaning the interior of the pot and lid with the palm sander. You can leave the interior unfinished; with use, the gourd shell will create its own natural sealer. Or, if you prefer, you can seal the inside of the pot and lid with melted paraffin, polyurethane, or salad bowl oil.

Scorched Tea Cups

These gourd cups are customarily used to drink maté, the green tea that is popular in South America. Some of the cups are very plain, but many are highly embellished, using silver and semiprecious stones. For everyday use, simple scorched designs help family members identify their own cups.
You can make a set with different patterns for family and guests. Maté cups used in Latin American countries are not sealed, and are often only crudely cleaned of gourd pulp.
For your personal use, however, be sure to clean the cups thoroughly, and either leave them plain or seal them with polyurethane.

YOU WILL NEED

Several gourds*

Gourd cleaning supplies

Pruning shears

Pencil

Small saw

Files and sandpaper

Small, hand-held butane torch

Polyurethane

Paintbrush

*Use small bottle gourds or the tops of large gourds.

1 Clean the outside of the gourds. Draw a line on one of the gourds to indicate where you will be cutting, and then cut the cup. If necessary, clip off the stem with pruning shears. Repeat this process to cut the other cups.

4 Use the butane torch to burn the outlines of the design. Tip: Practice on gourd scraps to perfect your scorching skills. Some gourd shells are softer than others, and therefore burn more easily. Experience will help you determine how close to hold the flame to the gourd, and how quickly to move it along the lines of the design.

2 Clean the interior of the cups thoroughly, removing all the pulp and seeds. File and sand the cut edges well: you want the cups to feel smooth against your lips.

5 Coat the interior of the cups with polyurethane. To seal the entire gourd, you can coat the outside with polyurethane, too. Let the cups dry.

3 Sketch a simple design on the exterior of the cups.

Branded Bracelets

This project makes great use of gourd scraps.
You simply cut rings from the tops of bottle gourds, making sure they are wide enough to fit over your
hand. The striking geometric design is easily achieved with a branding tip on a woodburning tool.
If the gourd shell is not especially strong, you can reinforce it by gluing a strip of
leather to the inside of the bracelet.

YOU WILL NEED

Gourd scrap about 9 to 10 inches (23 to 25 cm) in circumference

Hobby handsaw

Files and sandpaper

Woodburning tool with branding tip

Black acrylic paint or leather dye

Paintbrush

Clear varnish

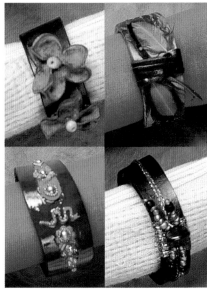

VARIATION:
COLORED NAPKIN RINGS

You can also make napkin rings using smaller gourd rings. You can woodburn the rings, or decorate them with paint, pods, beads, buttons, shells, old jewelry, ribbons, and feathers. Attach the decorative elements with glue, thread, or ribbon.

1 Select a gourd scrap with the right diameter to fit over your hand comfortably. Cut a ring that is at least 1 inch (2.5 cm) wide.

2 File the inner edges and sand smooth.

3 Use the branding attachment on the woodburner to create a design, using the photograph on page 48 as a guide, or create one of your own. These attachments come in a variety of shapes, including squares, diamonds, and circles.

4 Color the inside of the bracelet with paint or leather dye, and let dry.

5 Finish with several coats of varnish inside and out, and let dry. This will protect the design and strengthen the shell.

Top left: Dyan Mai Peterson, gourd musical instrument, woodburning, leather dyes, embellishments; top right: Carolyn Rushton, *Early Spring*, 5" high (13 cm) woodburned egg gourd, and *Native American*, 2½" high (6 cm) woodburned mini-bottle gourd; bottom right: Carol St. Pierre, woodburned and beaded necklace; bottom left: Carol Morrison, woodburned bracelets; all photos by Richard Hasselberg

Woodburned Bowls

These beautiful bowls, designed by Carol Morrison, look very complex, but the basic design is simple. The pattern can be used on gourds of different sizes to create eye-catching jewelry or large containers. Once you master the basic technique, experiment with variations on small gourds to create special gifts. The challenge in this project is to keep the woodburned lines even, since gourd shells often have harder and softer spots, much like the grain lines of wood.

YOU WILL NEED

Small gourd

Gourd cleaning supplies

Cup

Pencil

Foam pad

Small saw

Files and sandpaper

Hobby handsaw

Scrap of paper

Masking tape

Woodburner

Rubber or latex gloves

Dark brown or black shoe polish

1 Clean the outside of the gourd. Stabilize the gourd on the foam pad and cut off the top with the saw.

2 Mark a scallop shape on opposite sides of the gourd and cut them out with the hobby saw. Clean out the pulp and seeds. File and sand the cut edges.

3 Place a cup on top of the gourd, and use it to mark a ring around the top. This line will serve as a guide for drawing the horizontal lines of the design.

4 Tape a strip of paper to the gourd, and mark the placement of the remaining horizontal rows with short pencil lines first on the paper and then on the gourd. Move the strip of paper a fourth of the way around the gourd, and mark another set of lines in the same locations; repeat this process all around the gourd. Then connect the marks with horizontal lines.

5 Woodburn the horizontal lines all around the gourd. Be very careful to move the woodburning tool slowly and evenly along the marked line. Soft spots on the gourd shell may cause the tool to burn deeper in some sections than others. This project will give you plenty of practice keeping your lines even and straight!

6 After the horizontal lines are burned, mark and burn the vertical lines. Keep in mind that these lines will be closer together at the top and bottom than in the middle because of the curvature of the gourd.

7 To complete the design, follow the diagram shown here, filling in each square you have created.

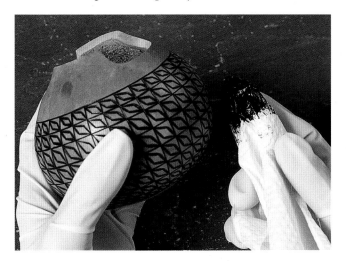

8 Once all the squares are filled in, use shoe polish to darken and protect the surface of the gourd.

These woodburned gourds are by Carol Morrison. So time consuming is this type of woodburning, that Carol calls her gourds "Slow Burn." The hours she spends provide relaxation and a precious zenlike tranquility. Photo by Richard Hasselberg

Leaf Motif Luminaria

This lovely lantern combines two simple techniques—cutting holes and woodburning. The openings in the gourd shell allow the candlelight to shine through. You can also use this design to hold potpourri. Fill the cut gourd with dried flowers and herbs and bring the sweet fragrance of nature into your home.

YOU WILL NEED

Gourd

Gourd cleaning supplies

Small saw

Files and sandpaper

Rubber band

Pencil

Leaf template

Hobby handsaw with a fine blade

Woodburner

Wood stain

Black acrylic spray paint

Paintbrush

Black permanent marker

Gold and black paint pens

Black or dark brown acrylic paint or leather dye

Fine-point paintbrush

1 Clean the outside of the gourd. Cut off the gourd neck, and remove the seeds and pulp. File and sand the cut edge. Find the center of the gourd by placing a rubber band around the middle of the gourd, and then drawing this line.

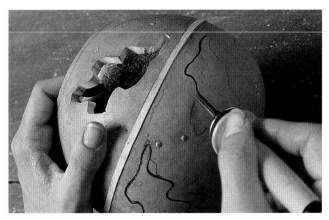

4 Woodburn around the outlines of the leaves in the lower half. Also woodburn a band around the center of the gourd and around the neck of the gourd.

2 Enlarge the leaf pattern (page 56) to fit your gourd, and then trace it onto the upper and lower halves of the gourd shell.

5 Brush on a coat of wood stain to cover the outside of the gourd, and let dry. Spray the interior of the gourd black.

3 Use the hobby saw to carefully cut out the leaves in the upper half of the shell.

6 Darken the gourd rim with the black marker.

7 Use dark brown or black acrylic paint or leather dye to darken the background of the lower half of the gourd, painting around the leaves.

8 With the gold paint pen, create metallic bands at the rim and the middle of the gourd. Paint the cut edges of the leaves gold to add a slight shimmer.

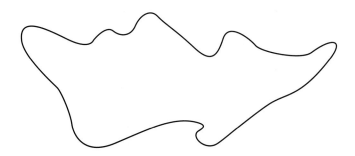

Denny Wainscott, *Starbird*,
6" diameter (15 cm) carved gourd,
wood stain and leather dyes,
photo by Richard Hasselberg

Pedestal Bowl with Decoupage Lining

Decoupage is an attractive way to finish the interior of a gourd bowl that may be discolored. Layers of decorative handmade paper and glue can also strengthen a weak or thin gourd shell, as well as hide a repair. Here, decoupage disguises the joinery used to create a pedestal bowl from two pieces of gourd. The bottom of the bowl is created by cutting a disk from a gourd scrap and gluing it to seal the bottom. You can leave the exterior of the gourd plain or you can decorate it with a pattern to match the design of the paper.

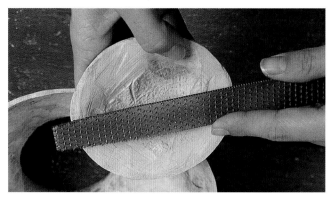

1 Select a bottle gourd that has a thin waist between two larger bulbs. The bulbs should be in a line so that the bowl will stand upright when cut and shaped. Cut both ends off the gourd, saving the middle section. Clean the outer gourd shell, and remove the pulp and seeds. Cut out a disk from the saved section that will completely seal the hole in the bottom of the bowl. File and sand the cut edges, and shape the disk for a snug fit.

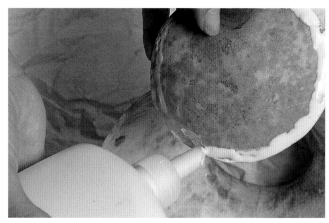

2 Apply glue to the rim of the gourd circle and glue it in place. Let dry.

The interior of this pedestal bowl was covered with two coats of textured paint to completely camouflage the joinery, then a simple design was woodburned around the rim.

3 Apply wood putty around the edge of the circle, protecting your hands with gloves. Let dry overnight. Sand the inside of the bowl thoroughly and wipe out the dust. Seal the inside of the bowl with varnish, and let dry.

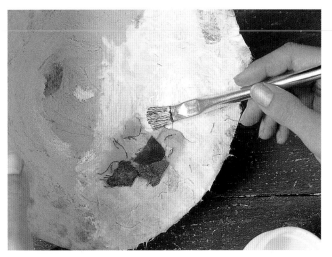

4 Tear the handmade paper into small pieces. If the paper is thick, you may need to wet it first; blot off the excess water, and then tear the paper into pieces. This technique creates nice, feathered edges.

5 Brush on a generous layer of decoupage medium.

6 Place pieces of paper on the sticky surface, and then apply another layer of medium. Overlap the pieces slightly to make sure the entire surface of the gourd is covered. Be sure to put a coating of medium on top of each piece of paper as you add it. When you are pleased with the arrangement, add a final coat of decoupage medium. Let the bowl dry overnight.

7 Spray the interior and exterior of the bowl with varnish to completely seal the surface.

Carved Vase

This lovely vase was made with hand-carving tools designed for use on wood, but they work very well on gourds. Be sure to protect the hand that is holding the gourd, since a gouge can slip off the surface of a round gourd shell. The gourd undershell is usually soft and rough, which provides an interesting design and texture contrast to the darker outer shell. You can highlight this distinction by staining the gourd before you begin to carve.

YOU WILL NEED
Gourd
Gourd cleaning supplies
Small saw
Foam pad
Sandpaper
Pencil
Small gouge
Fish fileting glove or supple leather glove*
Straightedge blade
Leather dye, shoe polish, or wood stain (optional)
Clear spray varnish

*The fish fileting glove is available at sporting goods stores.

1 Cut off the neck of the gourd. Clean the outside of the gourd, and remove the seeds and pulp. Sand the cut edge. Draw a design on the upper portion of the gourd with a pencil. Because gourds are always slightly irregular, patterns must be adjusted and adapted to the shape and size of the gourd. You can copy the pattern from this project or let the shape of the gourd suggest a different design.

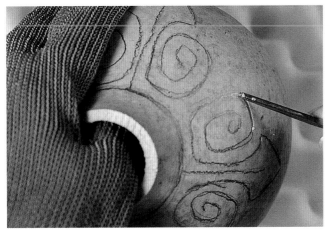

2 Stabilize the gourd on the foam pad, and hold the gourd in your gloved hand. Because the gourd surface can be quite slippery, begin by pushing the gouge straight down into the gourd shell. Then push with a gentle rocking motion to create a carved line. Tip: On a gourd scrap, practice holding the gouge at a constant angle so that the blade maintains a consistent depth. The curvatures of different blades will create thicker or thinner lines. Experiment with gourd scraps to find a blade that fits your design.

4 Use a straightedge blade to straighten or clean up some of the edges. Protect the exposed carved inner surface with a light spray coat of clear varnish. The carved gourd can be left plain at this point or finished with leather dye, shoe polish, or wood stain. The softer inner shell will absorb more of the dye and become darker than the outer shell.

Tip: To use this gourd as a vase for cut flowers, it's a good idea to slip a plastic liner inside the gourd.

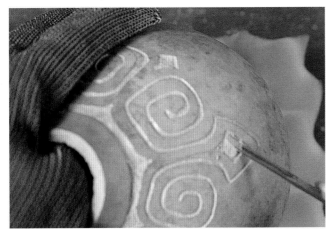

3 Parts of the design may require more of the outer shell to be removed. Use a gouge with a wider cutting edge to clear more of the shell.

Larry Sherman, carved gourd, leather dyes and wax, hand-chipped with 1-cm, u-shaped viner tool, photo by Sandra Stambaugh

Relief Carved Bowl

It takes a little more time to carve this attractive bowl, but the results are worth it! You can remove the top layer of the gourd shell around the design with hand tools or use a high-tech solution—a motorized cutting tool. Either way, your gourd will be linked in tradition to many world cultures that created similar relief carving on gourds.

YOU WILL NEED

Gourd

Gourd cleaning supplies

Small saw

Files and sandpaper

Copier paper

Scissors

Masking tape

Pencil

Design template

Carbon paper

Woodburning tool

Art gum eraser

Rubber or latex gloves

Medium brown leather dye

Paintbrush

Motorized hand cutting tool

Hand-carving tools

Black acrylic paint or leather dye

Gold paint pen

Spray varnish

1 Clean the outside of the gourd. Cut off the gourd neck and clean out the seeds and pulp. File and sand the edge. Cut a strip of paper 2 to 4 inches (5 to 10 cm) wide, long enough to fit around the circumference of your gourd (or tape strips of paper end to end). Fold the paper into fourths, unfold it, and mark each quarter with a pencil line.

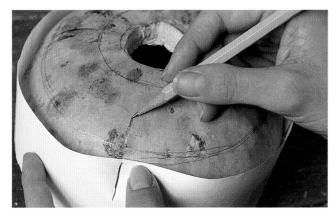

2 Tape the paper strip around the gourd. Mark the gourd with four pencil lines that correspond to the lines on the paper: you now have divided the gourd into four equal sections without having to do any math!

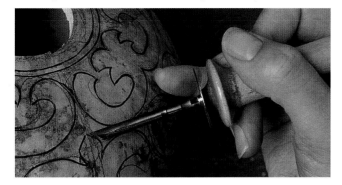

3 Enlarge the template so that it will fit on the top half of the gourd. Use carbon paper to transfer the design onto the gourd. Woodburn the design into the gourd shell. Also woodburn bands around the gourd opening and the middle of the gourd. Erase the pencil lines.

4 Brush leather dye on the gourd shell to completely color the upper half of the gourd. Let dry.

5 Use the motorized cutting tools or hand-carving tools to carve away the background on the top half of the gourd so that the woodburned design stands out in relief. Tip: If you are sensitive to gourd dust and the noise of the cutting tool, wear a dust mask and earplugs.

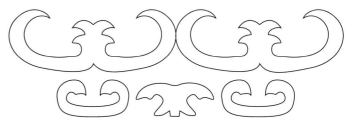

6 Use a smaller diameter rasp tip to create texture by lightly bouncing the tip on the carved background.

7 Paint or stain the bottom portion of the gourd black. Fill in the band around the gourd opening and the middle of the gourd with the gold paint pen. When the dye and paint are completely dry, spray varnish on the entire gourd to protect the surface.

Ginger Summit, carved gourd with leather dyes, photo by Sandra Stambaugh

Handled Basket with Leather Trim

This striking basket combines high-tech gourd-cutting techniques with traditional stitching. By covering the edges with lacing and leather, the gourd is reinforced, and will not chip or crack with continued use. The varnished interior helps to strengthen the gourd, as well as keep the surface clean. This basket, with its concho beads, is reminiscent of Southwest American basketry, and is both decorative and functional. Imagine yourself placing freshly picked flowers inside its ample opening!

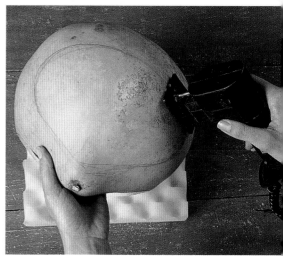

1 Clean the outside of the gourd. Mark the gourd where you will cut out the two sides to form the basket shape. Start the cut with a sharp knife, then use a power or hand saw to cut out the two sides (see page 12 for details about cutting with a power saw).

2 Remove all the seeds and pulp, and clean out the interior thoroughly. File and sand the interior and the cut edges. Varnish the inside, outside, and all the cut edges of the gourd. Let dry.

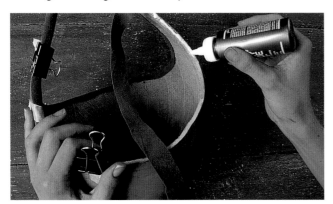

3 Cut leather strips approximately 1 to 1-1/2 inches (2.5 to 4 cm) wide, long enough to cover both cut surfaces of the basket. Glue in place. Use masking tape and binder clips to hold the leather in place while it dries overnight.

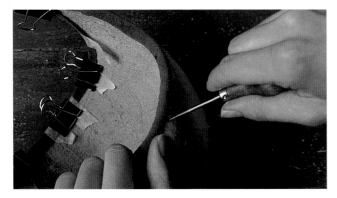

4 Use the awl to poke holes through the gourd, about 1 inch (2.5 cm) apart, right below the leather strip, all around the gourd rim.

5 Pull a leather thong halfway through one of the holes. Thread one end of the thong through each hole, angling the thong in one direction, until you run out of thong. Then, with the other end of the thong, go back through each hole, crossing the thong on top of the laced thong, to create a crisscross pattern. Continue in this way, stitching crisscross, until you have stitched the leather all around the gourd and the handle. To add a new thong, simply glue the short ends under the leather edging, and begin a new thong in the same hole.

6 Use the awl to poke two holes, closely spaced, on each side of the basket where you will be attaching the concho beads. Thread a short piece of thong through the holes, from the inside of the gourd to the outside, and tie a concho bead on each side of the gourd. Add extra thongs to create fringe. Slip a few beads onto the fringe to complete the embellishment.

Miniature Pots with Knotless Netting

Knotless netting has been used for centuries to protect gourd vessels and containers during prolonged use at home or in the fields. Today netting is used primarily as a decorative technique. By using waxed linen in different colors, accented with beads, the simple gourd can be transformed into a piece of art to wear or enjoy in your home. This little container can hold a tiny treasure, enhance a Christmas tree, or be worn on a leather thong as a bold necklace.

YOU WILL NEED

Small gourd

Gourd cleaning supplies

Small saw

Sandpaper

Beads, enough to fit around the rim of the gourd

Sewing needle

Waxed linen

Scissors

Cyanoacrylate glue

Permanent marking pen or leather dye

Top right: Waxed linen is available in a wide variety of colors and is wonderful to use for knotless netting. As the netting extends around the gourd, the slightly sticky thread hugs the shell without the need for tape to hold it in place while you are working.

1 Clean the outside of the gourd. Cut off the neck and remove the seeds and pulp. Sand the cut edge. Thread a 4-foot-length (1.2 m) of waxed linen through the needle; string on the beads at the other end. There should be enough beads to fit loosely around the neck of your gourd. Tie the strand of beads securely around the gourd neck, and clip off the end beyond the knot.

2 With the needle, go behind and between the first two beads.

3 Come out through the loop that has been created under the first bead. Continue going behind and between the beads with the needle and thread, emerging through the loop of thread under each bead; stitchery, this is known as the buttonhole or blanket stitch.

4 For the second row, place the needle in the loop that was created under the bead, and pull it through the loop of thread that is created under the stitch. Pull the loops evenly. If the thread is pulled too tight, it will distort both the stitches in the row above, and also the stitches in the row that is being created.

5 When you run out of thread and need to add more, simply begin weaving with a new thread, leaving the ends of the old and new thread to overlap. After stitching several more rows, go back and glue down the ends of those threads. Continue adding rows of netting. As the netting begins to extend beyond the widest part of the gourd bowl, it will pull tighter, cinching the netting firmly against the gourd. By pulling the stitches tighter and tighter, a spiral is created.

6 Finish off your netting at the bottom of the gourd, and hide the final thread end under the dense knotting. Darken the edge of the pot with marking pen or leather dye.

Gourd with Pine Needle Coiling

Basketmakers have long enjoyed embellishing gourds with natural materials, such as pine needles. This type of basketry is very simple to do; you can coil the pine needles in one layer to cover the edge of the gourd or build up the rim with many layers to create a more elaborate design. Other natural materials such as vines, date palm, and sea grass can be used in place of pine needles.

YOU WILL NEED

Gourd	Leather awl
Gourd cleaning supplies	Large tapestry needle
Foam pad	Artificial sinew
Saw	Pine needles
Files and sandpaper	Bucket of water
Plastic or latex gloves	Scissors
Wood stain, oak or natural	Spray varnish (optional)
Paintbrush	

The pine needle coiling on the gourd in the front has been sprayed with varnish to give it a sheen. This also protects the rough sheaths from being brushed off accidentally when they are dry.

1 Clean the outside of the gourd. Cut off the top of the gourd to create a bowl. Remove the seeds and pulp, clean the interior, and sand the cut edge. Color the outside of the gourd with wood stain, and let dry. Use the awl to poke holes along the upper edge of the bowl, about 1 inch (2.5 cm) apart. To prevent the gourd from cracking, support the gourd on the other side with your fingers, and poke the awl between them.

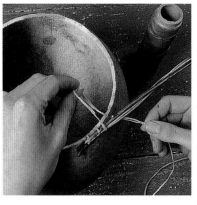

2 Soak the pine needles in water for about 30 minutes. Remove a few bundles, and blot off the excess water. Always work with damp pine needles. Begin by placing a small bundle of two or three tufts of pine needles along the rim. Thread the needle with sinew and knot one end. Insert the needle and sinew, starting inside the gourd, through the hole nearest to the pine needle bundle. Pull the thread taut, and then loop it over the pine needles.

3 Continue adding pine needles at regular intervals (i.e. every three stitches) so that the sheath or rough covering at the base of the needles forms a pattern.

4 If the bundle of pine needles gets too thick from the addition of new bunches, cut off some of the old needles from the back of the bundle; in this way you can keep the rows approximately the same diameter. To build up more layers, continue adding coils on top of those already secured.

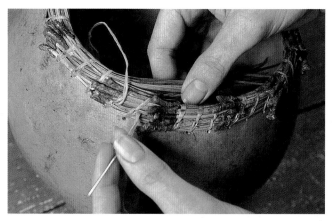

5 For the second layer, insert the tapestry needle in the lower row of pine needles rather than through the hole in the gourd. To finish off the coil, simply stop adding more pine needles, but continue to stitch down the existing ends. Trim off the ends at intervals so that gradually all of the needles are secured. Tie off the thread on the inside of the gourd. If you want, embellish the gourd with seeds, pods, or other attractive items from nature.

African Bead Shekerie

Gourds have been used as musical instruments for thousands of years in most countries around the world. One very popular instrument, which originated in Africa and was brought to the New World, is the shekerie, a rattle that has noisemakers fastened to a loose netting on the outside of the gourd. Noisemakers can be any small, hard object, including pods, seeds, shells, beads, and even buttons. Shekeries can range in size from small rattles to very large containers that are bounced from hand to hand. Tiny shekeries made with shiny beads make beautiful ornaments to wear or hang on a tree.

YOU WILL NEED

Lump in neck gourd

Gourd cleaning supplies

Drill with hole bit or small hobby saw

Sandpaper

Rubber or latex gloves

Brown leather dye

Scissors

Foam pad

Nail

Hemp, waxed linen, or linen flax

Bottle for gourd to sit on

Masking tape

Awl

Assorted beads*

*This gourd design used about 150 beads.

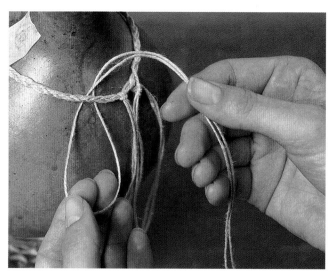

1 Clean the outside of the gourd. Drill a hole in the base about 2 inches (5 cm) in diameter. You can also make the hole with a small hobby saw. Clean out the seeds and pulp, and sand the cut edge. Color the exterior with brown leather dye, and let dry.

3 Cut 22 pieces of hemp, each 4 feet (1.2 m) long. To mount the first row of hemp, fold one strand in half and attach it to the ring with a lark's head or half-hitch knot. Pull to cinch tight around the anchor braid.

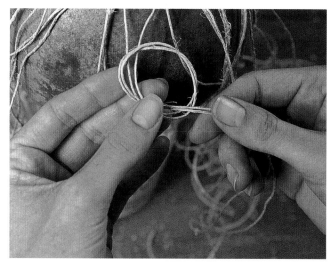

2 Push the nail into the foam pad. Cut two lengths of hemp, about 4 feet (1.2 m) long. Fold them in the middle, and place them around the nail. Make a braid long enough to loosely wrap around the neck of the gourd. Use the ends of the braid as part of the netting cords. Stabilize the gourd by sitting it on top of a bottle that has an opening slightly smaller than the diameter of the hole cut in the bottom of the gourd. Slip the braided hemp ring over the gourd neck and tape it to the gourd.

4 Using one strand from each of two pairs of adjacent cords in the first row, tie an overhand knot. You can adjust it to the correct position by tying the knot around the tip of the awl, and, while the knot is still loose, moving the awl to the place where the knot must be tightened or cinched.

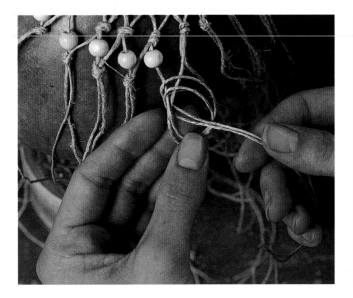

5 In the second row of knots, add a bead to one of each pair of cords, securing it in place with an overhand knot. Continue building the netting by adding beads as each knot is made.

7 When the netting has reached the bottom of the gourd, pull the ends of all the cords together, and tie in a single overhand knot.

6 Create your pattern by adding beads of different colors in each row. This shekerie design has eight rows of beads; yours may have more or less, depending on the size of your gourd, the density of the netting, and the size of the beads.

Karen Makal, *Shekerie Necklaces,* **2 to 2½" high (5 to 6 cm) gourds, waxed linen or crochet thread, glass beads, photo by Richard Hasselberg**

Top left: Carolyn Rushton, *Rose Basket*, woodburned bottle gourd, photo by Richard Hasselberg; top right: Judy M. Mallow, *Black Thorn Gourd*, bushel gourd, black thorn limbs, fabric and leather dye, photo by McKenzie Photography; center: Dyan Mai Peterson, baskets with pine needle rims, woodburned, dyed, carved, photo by Tim Barnwell; bottom right: Don Weeke, painted and carved gourd, couched with date palm, photo by Richard Hasselberg; bottom left: Dyan Mai Peterson, *Gourd Ladies*, woodburned, leather dyes, with pine needle rim, photo by Richard Hasselberg

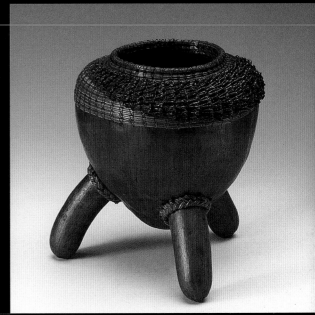

Top left: Jayne Stanley, (front) *Bridged Asymmetry*, bushel gourd, pine needles, waxed linen, nature-based stain, (back) *Whirlwind*, canteen gourd, pine needles, palm fibers, nature-based stain, photo by Richard Hasselberg; top right: Judy M. Mallow, *Gourd Vessel with Legs*, pine needles, leather dye, photo by McKenzie Photography; center: Linda Arias, *Australian Snake Pit*, painted snake gourds, photo by Richard Hasselberg; bottom left: Denny Wainscott, *Nigerian Design*, carved gourd with wood stain and leather dye, photo by Richard Hasselberg; bottom right: Judy M. Mallow, *Dyed Gourds*, 2" high (5 cm) and 4" high (10 cm) warty gourd centers, dyed pine needles, leather dye, photo by McKenzie Photography

Top left: Dyan Mai Peterson, *Gourd Hat*, woodburning, acrylic paints, pine needle coiled rim; top right: Carolyn Rushton, *Thunderbird Bowl*, woodburned kettle gourd; center: Ginger Summit, gourd with knotless netting and beads; bottom right: Linda Arias, cut poinsettia gourd bowl; bottom left: Marguerite Smith, *Baby Bobcats*, gourd with heavy woodburning and carving, acrylic paint, leather dye, photo by Paul Smith; all other photos by Richard Hasselberg

Contributing Artists

Mexican American gourd artist **LINDA ARIAS** is a member of the American Gourd Society, and a recipient of the Society's 1994 President's Award for the "Most Unusual Gourd" entry, among other awards. She also works with mosaics and tiles. She resides and works out of her "Gourd Art with Heart" Studio in Los Angeles, California.

LYNNE EVERETT is a contemporary basketweaver and gourd artist living in southern California. She teaches classes and workshops, sharing her knowledge of ancient techniques and tradition, while encouraging her students to feed the connections with the past.

JERRALDINE MASTEN HANSEN believes that the gourds she paints express her love of form and color, her appreciation of the Choctaw heritage that is her family legend, and her affinity for African and Japanese art. She lives in Carmel, California.

JANET HATFIELD discovered painted gourds while vacationing in New Mexico with her husband in 1992. She has been painting gourds with Native American designs ever since, under the watchful supervision of Jake the Wonderdog, from their home in Sunnyvale, California.

When **KAREN MAKAL** began selling gourds at the Gourd Factory, in Linden, California, where she lives, the idea that gourds were used as an art medium and for musical instruments came as something of a revelation. Soon she started using jewelry-size gourds to make ornaments and necklaces. Now she specializes in miniature shekeries.

JUDY MOFIELD MALLOW, a resident of Carthage, North Carolina, is a fifth-generation pine needle basketmaker whose work is displayed in museums and sold at many galleries and craft fairs. She is the author of *Pine Needle Basketry* (Lark Books, 1996), and runs her own mail-order business, Prim Pines, providing pine-needle basketry supplies to customers nationwide.

EILEEN MARCOTTE, through her business, Woven Wonders, located in Santa Cruz, California, creates and markets her unique gourds and baskets.

CAROL MORRISON discovered hardshell gourds many years ago in rural Ohio, where she grew up. A cultural anthropologist who specializes in the art of tribal people, she delights in discovering connections between her art and that of the many people she interacts with through her teaching and travels. Her gourd work features complex, woodburned geometrical designs. She lives in Palo Alto, California.

DYAN MAI PETERSON is a nationally known gourd artist and teacher. She enjoys experimenting with any size or shape of gourd that she can find or grow, to create decorative bowls, jewelry, and dolls. Her studio and home are located in Asheville, North Carolina.

CAROLYN RUSHTON is a gourd gardener, designer, and woodburning artist. She has worked with gourds for many years. She lives and works in Glenwood, Indiana.

CAROL ST. PIERRE is a gourd artist who lives and works in El Sobrante, California.

LARRY SHERMAN, a Professor of Educational Psychology at Miami University, in Oxford, Ohio, has been growing and crafting gourds for nearly 25 years. Annually he competes and shows his work at the Ohio Gourd Festival, the Kentucky Gourd Festival, and the Indiana Gourd Festival.

When **MARGUERITE L. SMITH** discovered gourds, she switched from painting on canvas to woodburning, carving, engraving, dying, and painting on gourds. She creates custom art pieces and participates in juried art shows. Endangered wild animals is the focus of much of her work, and she donates a portion of the sales from her Wild Animal Art series to Shambala and the Roar Foundation. She lives in Lancaster, California.

Through her business Gourdsket® Vessel Co. Inc., fiber artist **W. JAYNE STANLEY** creates and markets unique vessels that are part gourd, part basket. Her business is located in Broomfield, Colorado.

DENNY WAINSCOTT, a resident of Frankfort, Indiana, creates and markets his intricately carved pieces of art through his business, Morning New Gourds.

DON WEEKE is a gourd artist living in Julian, California. Although he experiments with a variety of surface techniques, he is best known for combining basketry with gourds, using natural materials in his environment.

Acknowledgments

Books are always the result of the talents and hard work of many people, and this work is no exception.

A special thanks to editor Deborah Morgenthal, who has been a champion of gourd crafters for many years. Her enthusiastic appreciation of the artists and their unique talents has greatly contributed to the dramatic increase in public awareness of this unusual and popular art form.

Thanks also to Rob Pulleyn and Carol Taylor for publishing this, my second book, on gourd crafts. The entire gourd community is greatly indebted to the vision of Lark Books.

Many thanks to the very talented members of the Lark staff whose combined efforts created a book that is beautiful in all its aspects. Art director Dana Irwin provided scrumptious settings for all the gourd projects, which were superbly photographed by Sandra Stambaugh. The informative how-tos were ably photographed by Richard Hasselberg. The steps in the projects were made much more attractive by the graceful hands of Catharine Sutherland.

A special tribute to all the artists who have so generously contributed examples of their work to inspire readers. Artists Janet Hatfield and Carol Morrison specifically designed projects for use in this book. More information on these and other artists can be found on page 77. This book is enriched by their willingness to share their talents and ideas with others.

And finally, a loving thanks to my husband Roger for once again being patient with a house filled with projects, notes, and conversations of gourds.

Index

A
Acrylic paints, 15, 22, 28, 31, 36, 39, 49, 54,
Artist's wax crayons, 27

B
Basketry, 65, 71-73
Birdhouses, 20, 39-41
Butane torch, 18, 46

C
Candleholders, 34
Carbon paper, 21
Carving, 18-19, 60-64
Christmas decorations, 22, 31
Cleaning gourds; the outside, 10; the inside, 11; with baking soda, 12, 20; with borax soap, 13
Coloring, 15-17; with color pigments, 15; with stains, inks, and dyes, 16; with wax and cream shoe polish, 16
Cracks, 13
Cucurbitaceae family, 8
Cutting, 11, with hand tools, 14; with power tools, 12

D
Decoupage, 13, 16, 57
Dimensional paints, 28
Dipper gourds, 28
Drying, 10

F
Finishes, 15, 19-20; for interior with food, 16-17, 20; for exterior, 19-20
Flowerpots, 24

G
Gourds; definition of, 8; history of, 7

H
Hardshell gourds, 9
Hemp, 71

I
Imperfections, 13
Insects, 13, 20

J
Jewelry, 13, 48, 67

K
Knotless netting, 67

L
Leather dyes, 22, 48, 54, 60, 71
Luffa sponges, 9

M
Mask, 26
Metallic paint pens, 22

O
Oil pastels, 43
Ornamental gourds, 9

P
Paraffin, 25, 45
Permanent markers, 26, 28, 36, 54
Pine needles, 69
Polyurethane, 20, 29, 45, 47

R
Repairs, 13
Rodents, 20
Rubber stamps, 21

S
Safety, 11, 12, 19, 20
Salad bowl oil, 28, 43
Sanding, 15
Scraps, 13
Shekerie, 71
Shoe polish, 24, 34, 51
Sponging, 33, 41

T
Tea cups, 46
Textured paint, 31, 58
Transferring a design, 21, 32, 37, 44, 63

V
Varnishes, 19-20, 33, 38, 41, 49, 59, 66, 69

W
Waxed linen, 67
Waxes, 19
Woodburning, 17, 44, 48, 51, 55, 63
Wood stain, 55, 60, 69

A Note About Suppliers

Usually, the supplies you need for making the projects in Lark books can be found at your local craft supply store, discount mart, home improvement center, or retail shop relevant to the topic of the book. Occasionally, however, you may need to buy materials or tools from specialty suppliers. In order to provide you with the most up-to-date information, we have created suppliers listing on our Web site, which we update on a regular basis. Visit us at www.larkbooks.com, click on "Craft Supply Sources," and then click on the relevant topic. You will find numerous companies listed with their web address and/or mailing address and phone number.